GOOGLE iQOO Z9x USER GUIDE

Comprehensive and Detailed Guide to Mastering the iQOO Z9x for Beginners.

By

Robert P. Mendez

Intentionally left blank

Table of contents

Intentionally left blank

INTRODUCTION

Greetings, and thank you for visiting our all-encompassing guide to mastering your Google iQOO Z9x! This user manual is intended to serve as your one-stop shop for all of the information that you need on your new smartphone, from the process of turning it on for the first time to the investigation of its technologically sophisticated capabilities. Your journey through the fascinating world of the iQOO Z9x will be facilitated by this guide, regardless of whether you are an experienced user of technology or a total novice.

A Peek into the World of Innovation

Within the realm of mobile technology, the Google iQOO Z9x is considered to be in the forefront. It sports a mix of strong hardware, smart software (courtesy of Google), and a feature-rich experience that will alter the way you use your phone. This comprehensive user guide covers every facet of the iQOO Z9x, ensuring that you are able to make the most of this exceptional gadget throughout its whole.

What You Come to Discover Within

The purpose of this detailed tutorial is to provide you with an in-depth understanding of your iQOO Z9x. It has been thoroughly developed. We will investigate:

Beginning with the unpacking of your phone and continuing on to the process of configuring it and customising it to your tastes is simple and straightforward.

Understanding the Hardware: A complete overview of the iQOO Z9x's physical components, including the display, camera system, buttons, and connectors.

Mastering the Software: A step-by-step tour through the Google operating system, covering everything from important applications and alerts to customizing settings and navigating the UI.

Unlocking Potential: Unveiling the iQOO Z9x's full potential with its sophisticated features including camera controls, game mode, multitasking capabilities, and Google-specific integrations.

Troubleshooting: A helpful hand for overcoming typical difficulties you could experience when using your phone.

Beyond the Basics

This article exceeds the simplest features of utilising your phone. We'll share useful insights on optimizing speed, maximizing battery life, using Google Assistant, and exploring the wonderful world of downloadable applications that will customise your iQOO Z9x experience even more.

Designed for Beginners

We recognise that not everyone is a computer guru. This user guide is developed with beginners in mind. We utilise plain and straightforward language, avoiding technical jargon wherever feasible. We'll give step-by-step tutorials with accompanying pictures to guarantee a smooth learning curve, regardless of your past familiarity with smartphones.

This user guide is thoughtfully prepared with over 2500 words devoted to providing you with thorough knowledge of your Google iQOO Z9x. With this guide on your side, you'll be well on your way to mastering every feature and function your phone has to offer.

Get Ready to Explore

The Google iQOO Z9x is a strong instrument begging to be explored. This user guide is your key to unlocking its potential and improving your mobile experience. So, dig in, discover the amazing features, and unleash the full potential of your Google iQOO Z9x!

CHAPTER 1

Welcome to the iQOO Z9x

Congratulations for being the happy owner of the iQOO Z9x! This intriguing smartphone is packed with features intended to improve your mobile experience. This chapter will walk you through the early stages of becoming acquainted with your new gadget, from the joy of unpacking to the critical configuration procedure.

Unboxing Your iQOO Z9x

The instant you get your iQOO Z9x, take a deep breath and appreciate the suspense! Carefully remove the outer packing and uncover the elegant box concealing your phone. Open the box to find the following treasures:

- Your brand new iQOO Z9x smartphone
- A charging adaptor suitable with your area
- A USB Type-C cable for charging and data transmission
- A user guide (you're already reading the complete version!)
- A SIM card ejector tool (if appropriate to your model)
- A warranty card (ensure you keep this document securely)

Depending on your area or purchasing package, you could also discover other products like a protective case, earbuds, or screen protectors.

Take a minute to appreciate the phone's design. Notice the beautiful contours, the brilliant display, and the strategically positioned buttons and ports. Familiarize yourself with the following physical elements of your iQOO Z9x:

Front: The huge display dominates the front, possibly covered by scratch-resistant Gorilla Glass or a comparable material. You could discover a cutout for the front-facing camera and a speaker grill at the top.

rear: The rear panel might be created from glass, plastic, or a mix of both. It could hold the back camera system together with an LED flash.

Sides: The sides often house the volume controls, power button, and a SIM card tray.

Bottom: The bottom edge may hold the USB Type-C charging connector and a speaker grill.

Top: There could be a 3.5mm headphone jack on the top (depending on the model).

Getting to Know Your Phone

Before delving into the setup procedure, let's review some of the important features of your iQOO Z9x:

Display: The iQOO Z9x has a gorgeous display, most likely an AMOLED screen giving brilliant colors, deep blacks, and high resolution. The size of the display might vary based on the model, but it's meant to give an immersive viewing experience for games, films, and daily usage.

CPU and RAM: The heart of your phone is the CPU, which performs all the computations and operations you throw at it. The iQOO Z9x is equipped with a strong CPU that, paired with its RAM (Random Access Memory), guarantees seamless performance while running programmes, multitasking, and playing games.

Storage: This is where you keep all your photographs, movies, applications, and data. The iQOO Z9x comes with a built-in storage capacity, which might vary based on the model you bought. If you require more space, you might be able to expand it further using a microSD card (check your model's specifications).

Cameras: The iQOO Z9x boasts a versatile camera system on the back, likely featuring multiple lenses for capturing stunning photos and videos in various lighting conditions. You'll also find a front-facing camera for selfies and video calls.

Battery: The iQOO Z9x is equipped with a long-lasting battery, allowing you to stay connected and powered throughout the day. The phone likely supports fast charging technology, enabling you to quickly replenish the battery when needed.

Operating System: Your iQOO Z9x runs on the Android operating system, offering a familiar and user-friendly interface. This software provides access to millions of apps, games, and customization options through the Google Play Store.

Powering On and Setting Up Your Device

Now that you're familiar with the phone's exterior and key features, it's time to power it on and embark on the setup journey. Locate the power button, usually situated on the right side of the phone. Press and hold the power button for a few seconds until the screen illuminates.

The initial setup process might involve choosing your preferred language, connecting to a Wi-Fi network, signing in with your Google account (which grants access to the Google Play Store and other services), and setting up a screen lock (like a PIN, fingerprint, or facial recognition) for added security.

You might be prompted to restore data from a previous phone or cloud backup if you choose. Otherwise, you can proceed with a fresh setup. The on-screen instructions will guide you through the remaining steps, which might include setting a date and time, enabling location services, and choosing preferred notification settings.

There's also a chance you'll encounter options for accessibility features, allowing you to customize the phone's interface and settings to suit your needs. This could include options for larger text, color inversion, or even voice control.

Connecting to the Network

A crucial step in the setup process is connecting your iQOO Z9x to a Wi-Fi network. Locate the Wi-Fi settings (usually found within the main settings menu) and choose the network you want to connect to. If it's a secure network, you'll need to enter the password. Once connected, your phone will have access to the internet, enabling you to download apps, access online services, and keep your software updated.

Adding a SIM Card

If your phone uses a SIM card (consult your user guide or retailer if unsure), it's time to insert it. Locate the SIM card tray using the provided SIM ejector tool. Carefully insert the tool into the designated slot on the phone's side and gently push until the tray pops out. Place the SIM card in the tray according to the provided markings, ensuring the correct orientation. Slide the tray back into the phone until it clicks securely in place.

Understanding Icons and Notifications

As you explore your phone, you'll meet several icons on the home screen and notification bar. These symbols indicate various programmes, functionalities, and notifications. Don't hesitate to touch and hold on a symbol to learn more about its function. Similarly, swiping down from the top of the screen displays the notification bar, showing notifications from applications, missed calls, and system messages. You may touch on a notice to get additional information or take action if required.

Taking a Tour with Google Assistant

Most likely, your iQOO Z9x comes pre-installed with Google Assistant, a smart voice assistant that can help you with numerous tasks. To activate it, just long-press the home button or use a specialised hotword trigger phrase (such "Hey Google" or "Ok Google"). Once triggered, voice your inquiry or command clearly. Google Assistant can help you make calls, create reminders, play music, search the web, and answer your questions in a natural, conversational manner.

By following these instructions, you've successfully turned on your iQOO Z9x and finished the basic setup procedure. You're now ready to explore the wide potential of your new smartphone. Don't hesitate to spend some time familiarizing yourself with the pre-installed apps and venturing into the Google Play Store to discover a world of customization options and functionalities. This comprehensive user guide will serve as your trusted companion as you delve deeper into the exciting world of your iQOO Z9x.

CHAPTER 2

Understanding the Android System

Your iQOO Z9x works on the Android system, a straightforward and user-friendly platform that powers millions of smartphones worldwide. This chapter digs into understanding the essential components of Android, allowing you to tailor your experience and unleash the full potential of your smartphone.

Navigating the Home Screen and App Drawer

The home screen is the centre focus of your Android experience. It's the first thing you see when you switch on your phone or hit the home button. This configurable area acts as a launchpad for your most-used programmes, widgets, and shortcuts.

Understanding Icons: The home screen is filled with app icons. These symbols reflect the numerous programmes loaded on your phone. Tapping an icon starts the related app. You may also press and hold on an icon to get more choices, such as uninstalling the programme, app details, or adding a widget to the home screen.

App Drawer: The app drawer holds all the applications installed on your phone, not simply those visible on the home screen. To access it, slide up from the bottom of the home screen. You may browse through the alphabetically listed applications or use the search box to discover a particular one.

Customizing the Home Screen

The brilliance of Android rests in its customisation capabilities. You may customise your home screen to suit your tastes and make it more effective for your everyday usage. Here's how:

Adding Apps and Widgets: Long press on an empty spot on the home screen. This frequently brings up a menu with choices like "Add widget" or "Add app." Widgets are mini-apps that give information or fast access to certain app features right on the home screen. For instance, a weather widget may show the current temperature and prediction.

Arranging Apps and Widgets: Tap and hold on an app or widget on the home screen. You may then drag and drop it to a different spot on the screen or another home screen page (if your phone allows multiple pages). Experiment to discover a layout that works best for you.

Creating Folders: For greater organising, you may organise related programmes into folders. Drag and drag one app on top of another app to create a folder. You may then rename the folder to anything useful, like "Social Media" or "Games."

Understanding the Dock

The dock is normally situated at the bottom of the home screen and may store a few app icons for easy access. You may add, delete, and rearrange programmes in the dock using the same drag-and-drop approach discussed before.

Using the Notification Panel and Quick Settings

The notification panel offers a single area for all your app alerts and system notifications. Swipe down from the top of the screen to access it. You'll get a list of alerts, including new emails, missed calls, social media updates, and more.

Interacting with Notifications: Tap on a notification to get additional information or take action. You may dismiss alerts by swiping them left or right. Some alerts enable you to respond straight from the panel without launching the app.

Clearing All alerts: If your notification panel is overflowing, you can normally touch a "Clear All" button at the bottom to dismiss all alerts at once.

Accessing Quick Settings

Swiping down twice from the top of the screen (or swiping down with two fingers on certain models) extends the notification panel to expose fast settings tiles. These tiles enable one-tap access to commonly used settings including Wi-Fi, Bluetooth, airplane mode, flashlight, and screen brightness.

Customizing fast Settings

You may normally change the fast settings panel by pressing on the "Edit" button (usually situated at the bottom). This enables you to rearrange the current tiles or add new ones depending on your preferences.

Customizing Your Phone's Look and Feel

Android provides a variety of choices to customise the appearance and feel of your phone, enabling you to create a unique user experience.

Changing the Wallpaper: The wallpaper is the background picture shown on your home screen. You may change it to a picture from your gallery, a pre-loaded wallpaper, or download one from the web. To set a new wallpaper, head to your phone's settings and search for choices like "Wallpaper" or "Display."

Themes: Some phone makers, notably iQOO, could provide downloaded themes that modify the whole appearance and feel of your phone's interface, including wallpapers, icons, and fonts. Explore the theme choices inside your settings to find different designs.

Launchers: While the home screen experience is pre-determined by your phone's manufacturer, you may download different launcher applications from the

Google Play Store. These launchers provide even more customization possibilities, enabling you to entirely change the look and functionality of your home screen.

Customizing Sounds and Notifications

Android enables you to modify the noises and notification alerts associated with your phone's activities and applications.

Ringtones and Notifications: Navigate to your phone's settings and search for "Sound" or "Notifications." Here you may modify the ringtone for incoming calls, notification sounds for various applications, and set the volume levels. You may also define unique notification sounds for individual applications.

Vibrations: You may change the vibration patterns for incoming calls, alerts, and when you touch the screen. This might be handy for instances when you might prefer muted notifications.

Fonts and Display Settings

Font Size and Style: For improved reading, you may alter the font size used throughout the Android system. Additionally, some phones can enable you to alter the system font style altogether.

Display options: Android provides several display options to tailor your viewing experience. You may adjust the screen brightness, enable night mode (which minimises blue light output for better sleep), and alter the screen timeout length (the time it takes for the screen to switch off after inactivity).

Taking Advantage of Accessibility Features

Android has a broad variety of accessibility features meant to cater to people with diverse requirements. These features may be accessed under the settings menu and comprise choices like:

Screen magnification: This enlarges the material on your screen, making it easier to view.

TalkBack: This function gives vocal feedback for everything that occurs on your screen, helping visually challenged individuals to manage their phones with ease.

Color correction: This alters the color display on your phone to increase visibility for those with color blindness.

By exploring these customization possibilities, you may change your iQOO Z9x into a device that exactly matches your personality and interests. Feel free to explore and find what works best for you. The beauty of Android resides in its versatility, enabling you to personalise the user experience to your individual requirements and aspirations.

CHAPTER 3

Making Calls and Texting - Staying Connected with Your iQOO Z9x

Your iQOO Z9x is more than simply a fantastic entertainment gadget; it's a critical communication tool. This chapter digs into the key features of making calls and sending text messages, helping you keep connected with friends, family, and coworkers.

Using the Phone App to Make and Receive Calls

The Phone app is the core of your calling experience on the iQOO Z9x. It's normally pre-installed and immediately accessible on your home screen or app drawer.

Making Calls: Launch the Phone app. You'll normally see a keypad displayed. Use the keyboard to input the phone number you wish to call. You may also access your contacts list by pressing on the "Contacts" option (typically found at the bottom of the screen). Once you have the appropriate number dialed, touch the "Call" button (typically a green phone symbol) to begin the call.

During a call, you may utilise the on-screen buttons to mute the microphone, engage loudspeaker, or access extra options like call hold or transfer.

Receiving Calls

When someone calls you, your phone will ring and show the caller's details (if accessible) on the screen. You'll see choices to answer the call (usually a green button) or refuse it (often a red button).
Swiping right on the answer button normally connects you to the call, whereas swiping left rejects it.

Managing Your Call History

The Phone app retains a record of your recent calls, including missed calls, outgoing calls, and received calls. You may view this history by pressing on the "Recent" tab (typically found at the bottom of the screen). This list enables you to swiftly return missed calls or check the contents of earlier talks.

Saving Contacts: Frequently contacting the same numbers? Save them to your phone's contact list for fast and handy access. You may access the contacts app from the Phone app or as a standalone app on your phone.

Speed Dial: Assign particular numbers to your speed dial for one-touch calling to your most critical contacts. Consult your phone's user guide or explore the options inside the Phone app to discover how to set up fast dial.

Sending and Receiving Text Messages with the Messaging App

The Messaging software, commonly pre-installed as "Messages" or a similar moniker, is your gateway to text messaging on the iQOO Z9x. This useful application enables you to exchange text messages (SMS) and multimedia messages (MMS) with your contacts.

Composing a New Text: Launch the Messaging app. Tap on the "New message" symbol (typically a plus sign or a message bubble icon). In the "To" area, enter the phone number or pick a person from your list. You may also send messages to numerous recipients by adding them all to the "To" column.

Compose your text message in the appropriate text area at the bottom of the screen. You may also add emojis, stickers, or even photographs and videos using the on-screen choices (these options could vary depending on your phone type). Once your message is ready, touch the "Send" button (typically an arrow icon) to transmit it to the recipient(s).

Receiving and Managing Text Messages
When you get a new text message, a notice will show on your screen, providing the sender's details and a preview of the

message. You may touch on the notice to read the message and see its complete text.

The Messaging app retains a record of all your text message chats. You may access them by launching the app and navigating through the list of discussions.

Additional Messaging Features

The Messaging app includes several capabilities beyond regular text messaging. Here are several to explore:

Group Chats: Communicate with numerous individuals concurrently by forming a group chat. Simply add all the relevant recipients to a new message and name your group for better identification.

MMS (Multimedia Messaging Service): Not restricted to text, you may also share multimedia information like images, movies, and voice recordings with MMS. Be advised that data costs can apply depending on your cell plan.

Emojis and Stickers: Express yourself artistically with a large collection of emojis and stickers accessible inside the Messaging app.

Using Additional Calling Features

The iQOO Z9x provides extra features beyond simple calling and messaging, giving you with greater control over your communication experience.

Call Waiting: This function enables you to receive a second incoming call while you're currently on a call. You may then opt to answer the new call, put the existing call on hold, or refuse the new call completely. Activating or disabling call waiting normally requires accessing your phone's call settings.

Voicemail: This function takes over when you miss a call or your phone is unavailable. Callers may leave a voicemail message, which you can recover later. To access your voicemail, call the voicemail number supplied by your carrier (usually 1 voicemail). You may then listen to your messages, store them, or delete them.

Call Forwarding: This function transfers incoming calls to another phone number, such as your voicemail or another mobile device. Call forwarding may be enabled to divert all calls, just unanswered calls, or busy calls. Activating or disabling call forwarding is normally done via your phone's call settings (see to your user guide for particular methods).

Do Not Disturb: This mode silences your phone's alerts and calls, offering you some peace and quiet. You may configure Do Not Disturb mode to accept calls from specified contacts or let calls through after a set number of rings. Activating or disabling Do Not Disturb mode may be done using the quick settings panel or dedicated settings menu on your phone.

Conference Calling: Engage in a discussion with numerous individuals simultaneously utilising conference calling. This functionality can involve starting the conference call using the Phone app or utilising a special service supplied by your carrier. Consult your user guide or carrier information for further instructions on conference call capability.

By familiarizing yourself with these extra functionalities, you can exploit the full potential of your iQOO Z9x's communication capabilities. Remember to explore your phone's settings and check your user guide for precise instructions and choices connected to these features, since they could differ somewhat depending on your phone type and carrier.

This chapter has prepared you with the fundamental information for making calls, sending text messages, and accessing extra calling options on your iQOO Z9x. Now you're ready to connect and interact with ease.

CHAPTER 4

Connecting to the Web and Staying Social - Expanding Your Horizons with the iQOO Z9x

Your iQOO Z9x is a portal to the huge world of the internet. This chapter offers you with the skills to connect to Wi-Fi networks, control mobile data use, and explore the fascinating domain of social media, keeping you informed and connected.

Wi-Fi Connectivity and Management

Wi-Fi is a wireless networking technology that enables your iQOO Z9x to connect to the internet at fast rates. Connecting to a Wi-Fi network is vital for downloading applications, viewing internet content, and keeping your software updated.

Finding and Connecting to Wi-Fi Networks

Swipe down from the top of the screen to open the notification panel.
Locate the Wi-Fi icon (typically represented by wavy lines) and press to turn Wi-Fi on (if it's not already enabled).
Your phone will search for accessible Wi-Fi networks in your neighbourhood. A list of networks will emerge, indicating their names and signal strengths.
Select the chosen network. If it's a secure network, you'll be requested to enter the password.

Once you input the right password and connect, your phone will be online and ready to browse the internet via Wi-Fi.

Managing Saved Networks: Your iQOO Z9x remembers previously connected Wi-Fi networks. This enables for automatic reconnection when you're in range of a familiar device. To manage stored Wi-Fi networks, browse to your phone's Settings menu. Look for choices like "Wi-Fi," "Network & internet," or similar.

In the Wi-Fi settings, you may examine a list of stored networks, update their passwords, forget undesired networks, or establish a favourite network for your location.

Advanced Wi-Fi functions: Some iQOO Z9x versions can include extra Wi-Fi functions including Wi-Fi hotspot capability. This enables your phone to operate as a portable router, sharing its internet connection with other devices like laptops or tablets. Consult your user handbook for precise information on activating and utilising a Wi-Fi hotspot.

You could also see choices for controlling metered Wi-Fi connections. This is significant if you have a restricted data plan connected with a particular Wi-Fi network. Your phone may be set to restrict background data consumption or inform you before exceeding a data limit on a metered connection.

Setting Up Mobile Data and Understanding Network Speeds

Mobile data lets your iQOO Z9x to access the internet while you're beyond the range of a Wi-Fi network. This data consumption is taxed by your cell carrier, therefore knowing data plans and network speeds is vital.

Activating Mobile Data: Similar to Wi-Fi, enter the notification panel by swiping down from the top of the screen.

Locate the Mobile Data symbol (typically represented by mobile network towers) and press to turn it on (if it's not already enabled). Turning on mobile data enables your phone to utilise your cellular network for internet access.

Understanding Mobile Data consumption

Be cautious of your mobile data consumption, particularly if you have a restricted data plan. Most carriers provide data use monitors that enable you to monitor your data consumption. You may normally retrieve this information via your carrier's app or web site.

Your phone's settings menu could also give choices for checking your mobile data consumption and setting data usage alerts or limitations.

Network Speeds: Mobile data networks come at different speeds, often signified by technical jargon like 3G, 4G, or 5G (depending on your carrier's coverage and your phone's capabilities). These words indicate distinct generations of cellular network technology, with each generation bringing greater data rates and enhanced performance.

5G is the newest and fastest mobile network technology, however its availability relies on your location and carrier's infrastructure. Consult your carrier for details about their network coverage and data package possibilities.

Using Social Media Apps and Staying Connected

Social networking applications have become a vital aspect of contemporary communication. They enable you to connect with friends and family, exchange updates, follow your hobbies, and discover new things.

Popular Social networking applications: There's a large assortment of social networking applications accessible on the Google Play Store. Some of the most popular ones are Facebook, Instagram, Twitter, TikTok, and Snapchat. Each app provides distinct features and caters to various interests.

Downloading and Installing Social Media Apps

Open the Google Play Store app on your iQOO Z9x. Search for the preferred social networking app by name in the Play Store's search box. Browse through the app's information page, including screenshots, ratings, and reviews. This might help you assess whether the app corresponds with your interests.

If you're persuaded, press the "Install" button. You may need to check in using your Google account or establish a new account for the individual app.

Once installed, the app icon will display on your home screen or app drawer. Launch the app and create a profile or sign in using your current account information.

Navigating Social Media applications
Social media applications often have certain basic functionality despite their individual features. Here's a general overview

Creating a Profile: Most social networking applications ask you to create a profile, which generally includes a username, profile photo, and a brief bio.

Following and Connecting with Others: Search for friends, relatives, or individuals who share your interests. You may follow their profiles to view their posts and updates.

Posting Content: Share your opinions, experiences, or discoveries by posting posts. These updates may contain text, photographs, videos, or even live streaming (depending on the programme).

Liking and Commenting: Engage with other users' material by liking their posts or posting comments.

Direct Messaging: Many social networking programmes include private messaging services, enabling you to engage one-on-one chats with other users.

Social Media Etiquette: The world of social media feeds on courteous conversation. Here are some fundamental social media etiquette tips:

- Be wary of what you publish. Once anything is online, it might be impossible to delete altogether.
- Be polite towards others, even when you disagree.
- Avoid publishing private information about yourself or others.

- Be conscious of your privacy settings and alter them to your comfort level.

By following these steps and keeping social media etiquette in mind, you may utilise the potential of social media applications to interact with people, share your experiences, and remain informed about the world around you. Remember, the beauty of social media rests in its potential to develop relationships and form communities. Use it carefully and have fun exploring the huge social environment it provides!

This chapter has prepared you with the skills to connect to the web via Wi-Fi and mobile data, analyse network speeds, and navigate the fascinating domain of social networking applications. With your iQOO Z9x in hand, you're now ready to explore the endless possibilities of the internet and remain connected with the world around you.

CHAPTER 5

Unveiling the Camera's Potential

The iQOO Z9x offers a strong camera system, letting you to shoot breathtaking photographs and movies of your environment. This chapter digs into the camera app's UI, shooting modes, and critical settings, changing you from a casual snapper to a photography connoisseur.

Exploring the Camera App Interface and Shooting Modes

Launching the camera app on your iQOO Z9x unleashes a world of creative possibilities. Let's browse the UI and investigate the different shooting modes.

The Camera App Interface: The layout could change somewhat based on your exact model, however most camera applications share fundamental aspects. Here's a broad overview:

Viewfinder: The huge middle section offers the live preview of what your camera views. This is where you frame your photographs.

Capture Button: The most visible button, generally positioned at the bottom of the screen, begins picture or video capture. A single push takes a snapshot, whereas a lengthy press frequently begins video recording.

Shooting Modes: Various shooting modes adapt to diverse scenarios and creative demands. These modes are often accessible by swiping left or right on the screen (or by a dedicated mode button) and could contain choices like Photo, Portrait, Video, Night Mode, and more.

More Controls: Several more controls surround the viewfinder and capture button. These controls could vary based on the shooting mode but commonly include choices for:

Flash toggle: Turn on/off the flashlight for low-light scenarios.

HDR (strong Dynamic Range) Capture images with balanced exposure in scenarios with strong contrast.

Zoom: Enlarge your subject using digital zoom (be mindful that excessive zoom will impair picture quality).

Gallery shortcut: Quickly access your captured photographs and videos.

Settings button: Access sophisticated camera settings for more comprehensive control over your images.

Understanding Shooting Modes: The iQOO Z9x provides a range of shooting modes to suit to diverse conditions. Here are some common ones:

Photo: The basic option for photographing ordinary scenes.

Portrait: Ideal for taking portraits with a blurred backdrop effect, showcasing your subject.

Video: Record high-quality videos for documenting memories or producing your own content.

Night Mode: Enhances low-light photography by capturing brighter and sharper photographs in dark conditions.

Pro Mode: Unlocks manual controls over parameters like shutter speed, ISO, and white balance, allowing additional creative flexibility for skilled users.

Capturing Photos and Videos with Essential Settings

Before entering into creative exploration, let's examine some fundamental options to increase the quality of your images and movies.

Adjusting Resolution: Most camera programmes enable you to adjust the picture or video resolution. Higher resolutions result in crisper photos and higher file sizes. Choose a resolution that balances quality and storage capacity.

Exposure Compensation: This parameter influences the overall brightness of your shot. Use it to adapt for extremely bright or dark situations. A positive number brightens the picture, whereas a negative value darkens it.

Focus: Ensure your topic is crisp and in focus. Tap on the region of the viewfinder where you wish the camera to concentrate. Some camera applications include settings for continuous focusing, monitoring a moving target.

Using the Flash: The flash may be beneficial in low-light circumstances, but be cautious of sharp shadows it could generate. Your camera app could provide multiple flash options like Auto, On, Off, and

Red-Eye Reduction (which helps eliminate red-eye in portraiture).

Taking Stunning Photos in Different Lighting Conditions

Lighting plays a critical part in generating engaging images. Let's review some techniques for conquering diverse lighting settings with your iQOO Z9x camera:

Capturing in Bright sunshine: Bright sunshine may cause to harsh shadows and washed-out hues. Try using HDR mode to balance the exposure or increase exposure compensation slightly to darken the picture. You may also employ shade to provide more even illumination.

Low-Light Photography: Low-light settings might result in blurry or grainy images. Utilize Night Mode for increased low-light performance. If Night Mode isn't available, consider using a tripod for picture stabilization and modify exposure compensation to brighten the image (be cautious of increasing noise at higher exposure settings).

Utilizing Portrait Mode: Portrait mode offers a very beautiful backdrop blur effect, letting your subject stand out. Ensure good lighting and keep a modest gap between yourself and the subject for maximum results.

Playing with Composition: The way you organise objects inside the frame is vital for captivating images. Here are some fundamental composition suggestions to consider:

Rule of Thirds: Imagine splitting the viewfinder into a 3x3 grid. Position your subject along the connecting lines or at the spots where the lines meet for a more balanced composition.

Leading Lines: Use natural lines in your area, such a road or a river, to attract the viewer's attention into the frame and towards your subject.

Negative Space: Don't fill the frame totally. Leaving some vacant space surrounding your topic may provide a feeling of balance and underline the subject's significance.

By learning these basic settings and approaches, you'll be well on your way to creating great images and movies with your iQOO Z9x camera in varied lighting circumstances. Remember, practice makes perfect! Experiment with various shooting modes, settings, and compositions to find your own style and convert daily events into memorable memories.

This chapter has prepared you with the knowledge to browse the camera app, explore shooting modes, modify critical settings, and produce appealing photographs in varied lighting circumstances. With your gained talents and the powerful camera system of the iQOO Z9x, you're ready to go on a voyage of photographic discovery and capture the world around you in a whole new light!

CHAPTER 6

Multimedia on the iQOO Z9x

Your iQOO Z9x is more than simply a communication and productivity tool; it's a multimedia powerhouse. This chapter discusses the numerous methods to consume music, films, and other media files on your smartphone.

Playing Music and Videos with Built-in Apps

The iQOO Z9x comes pre-installed with key programmes for playing music and movies. Let's look into these built-in apps.

Music Player: Locate the Music Player app on your home screen or app drawer. This programme enables you to play music files saved on your phone's internal storage or microSD card (if your phone supports expandable storage). The Music Player normally organizes your music collection by artist, album, genre, or playlist. You may browse your music library and touch on a song to start playing.

Most Music Player applications feature basic playing options like play/pause, skip forward/backward, and volume adjustment. You could also discover options like shuffle and repeat capabilities for personalised listening experiences.

Video Player: Similar to the Music Player, your iQOO Z9x likely features a pre-installed Video Player programme. This programme enables you to play numerous video types saved on your smartphone.

The Video Player software organizes your video collection, enabling you to browse and pick films for playing. Playback features like play/pause, fast forward/rewind, and volume adjustment are frequently accessible. Some Video Player applications include extra capabilities like subtitle support and the option to modify screen brightness or playing speed.

Downloading and Using Streaming Services

While pre-installed applications cater to locally stored material, the world of streaming services provides large libraries of music, movies, TV series, and more, available on-demand with an internet connection.

Popular Streaming Services: A variety of streaming services are available for download on the Google Play Store. Some popular alternatives are Spotify, YouTube Music, Apple Music (if compatible), Netflix, Hulu, Disney+, and HBO Max (depending on your location and service availability).

Downloading Streaming Apps

Open the Google Play Store app on your iQOO Z9x.

Search for the preferred streaming service by name in the Play Store's search box.

Browse through the app's information page, including screenshots, ratings, and reviews.

If you're persuaded, press the "Install" button. You may need to login in with your current account or establish a new account for the particular streaming provider.

Once installed, the app icon will display on your home screen or app drawer. Launch the app and login in using your account credentials to access the streaming library.

Membership Options: Most streaming services demand a membership to access their complete content catalogue. Subscription rates vary based on the service and the selected plan (individual vs. family plans, ordinary vs. premium plans with greater quality streaming).

Transferring Media Files Between Devices

There are various methods to transfer media files between your iQOO Z9x and other devices.

Using a USB connection: The most frequent way is connecting your iQOO Z9x to a computer using a USB connection. Your phone might prompt you to allow data transfer when connected. On your computer, navigate to your phone's storage using the file explorer. You can then drag and drop media files between your computer and your phone's storage.

Bluetooth Transfer: If both devices support Bluetooth file transfer, you can utilize Bluetooth for media sharing. Enable Bluetooth on both your iQOO Z9x and the receiving device. Locate the media files you want to transfer on your iQOO Z9x and initiate the sharing process through the file manager app (or the specific app where the media is located). Select Bluetooth as the transfer method and choose the receiving device from the list of available Bluetooth connections.

Cloud Storage Services: Cloud storage services like Google Drive, Dropbox, or OneDrive offer online storage space. You can upload your media files to the cloud storage and then access them from any device with an internet connection and the corresponding cloud storage app installed. This method is convenient for transferring media files wirelessly and also creates a backup of your files in the cloud.

By understanding these methods, you can seamlessly transfer your favorite music, videos, and other media files between your iQOO Z9x and other devices, ensuring you have your entertainment library at your fingertips whenever you need it.

This chapter has equipped you with the knowledge to play music and videos using built-in apps, explore the world of streaming services, and transfer media files between devices. With your iQOO Z9x and its multimedia capabilities, you're now prepared to turn everyday commutes, leisure moments, and travel adventures into journeys filled with music, laughter, and captivating entertainment. Remember, the possibilities are endless – explore different genres, discover new artists, and curate your own personalized multimedia experience on your iQOO Z9x.

CHAPTER 7

Gaming on the iQOO Z9x - Unleashing the Power for Epic Gameplay

The iQOO Z9x has amazing hardware built to give a seamless and immersive gaming experience. This chapter prepares you to improve your phone's performance, investigate game-specific features (if available on your model), and handle gaming data properly.

Optimizing Performance for a Smooth Gaming Experience

Before plunging into the realm of mobile gaming, let's examine some methods to improve your iQOO Z9x for a flawless and fun experience.

Battery Optimization: Mobile games may deplete your battery rapidly. Navigate to your phone's battery settings and seek for choices like "Battery optimization" or "App power management." You may isolate gaming applications from battery optimization to guarantee they get maximum power when playing. Be warned that this can contribute to quicker battery depletion overall.

Background App Refresh: Running numerous programmes in the background will eat resources and possibly slow down your game performance. Consider reducing background app refresh, particularly for applications you're not actively using while gaming. Background app refresh options may often be located inside your phone's settings menu.

Game Mode (if available): Some iQOO Z9x models could offer a specific "Game Mode." This mode optimizes phone settings including network priority, performance profiles, and notification filtering to maximise your gaming experience. Explore your phone's settings to see whether a Game Mode option is available and enable it for an additional performance boost during games.

Graphics options (inside games): Many games include in-app graphics options. These options enable you to change visual quality (resolution, textures) and frame rate. Experiment with these settings to achieve a balance between outstanding images and smooth performance on your iQOO Z9x. Prioritize a higher frame rate for a more responsive gaming experience, even if it means losing some graphical elements.

Display Settings: Consider tweaking your display settings for best gameplay. Some iQOO Z9x versions could have a high refresh rate display. A high refresh rate helps for smoother images during fast-paced action. Enable the maximum refresh rate your phone supports if available inside the display settings menu. Additionally, you could see choices for increasing screen brightness or setting features like "Do not disturb" mode to limit distractions while gaming.

Utilizing Game-Specific Features (if available)

Some iQOO Z9x models could come bundled with game-specific features meant to improve your gaming. These characteristics may vary based on your exact model, but here are some examples:

Touch Enhancements: Features like "Game touch acceleration" or "Pressure sensitive touch" may boost touch responsiveness and accuracy during gaming, giving you an advantage in fast-paced games.

In-Game Assistant: A virtual assistant could be offered inside certain games, giving rapid access to controls, snapshots, or screen recordings without leaving the game.

4D Game Vibration: Enhanced vibration feedback coordinated with in-game activities may offer a more immersive gaming experience (if supported by your model).

Explore the options inside your games or check your phone's user guide to uncover any game-specific features your iQOO Z9x could provide. Utilizing these elements may boost your gaming and offer a more competitive edge.

Managing Game Data and Storage

Mobile games may amass enormous quantities of data, including game files, downloadable material, and save data. Here's how to successfully manage game data and storage on your iQOO Z9x:

Understanding Storage Usage: Navigate to your phone's storage settings. Look for a section that indicates storage consumption by app. This helps you to detect games that are taking a considerable quantity of storage space.

Clearing Game Cache: The game cache contains temporary data that might build over time. Clearing the game cache might possibly free up storage space without harming your game saves or progress. The option to remove the game cache may often be found inside the app settings for the individual game in your phone's app management menu.

Moving Game Data to SD Card (if applicable): If your iQOO Z9x supports expandable storage via a microSD card, you may move game data to the SD card to free up space on your phone's internal storage. This option can be accessible inside the app administration menu for the individual game or within your phone's storage settings. Moving huge game files to the SD card will reduce loading speeds marginally, but be aware that certain games might not run adequately when loaded on external storage.

Removing Games: If you no longer play a game, try removing it to regain substantial disc space.

Uninstalling a game often destroys all related game data, including save files and downloadable material. Before uninstalling, check you've backed up your game progress if cloud save options are offered inside the game itself. Uninstalling games may be done using the app management section inside your phone's settings.

Cloud Gaming Services (optional): Cloud gaming services like Google Stadia or Microsoft xCloud enable you to stream high-end games straight to your phone without downloading massive game files. This may be a realistic alternative for testing out new games or playing resource-intensive titles without filling up your phone's storage. However, cloud gaming services demand a solid internet connection with significant bandwidth for best performance.

By following these recommendations for maximising speed, discovering game-specific features, and managing game data properly, you can make your iQOO Z9x into a powerful gaming machine. Remember, practice makes perfect!

Experiment with various games and settings to find what works best for you and unleash your inner champion on the mobile gaming arena. With the iQOO Z9x in your hands, you're ready to conquer virtual worlds, dominate leaderboards, and experience the excitement of mobile gaming at its best.

CHAPTER 8

Unlocking the Power of Performance

Your iQOO Z9x is a powerhouse engineered for smooth performance and efficient multitasking. This chapter goes into understanding major components that effect performance - RAM, storage, and battery life. We'll also discuss techniques to optimize your phone for common chores and increase battery life for a really optimised user experience.

Understanding RAM, Storage, and Battery Life

Three important components greatly impact your iQOO Z9x's performance:

RAM (Random Access Memory): Think of RAM as your phone's short-term memory. It retains previously used data and programmes for rapid retrieval, enabling you to transition between activities easily. More RAM often correlates to easier multitasking and quicker programme loading times.

Storage: This refers to the long-term storage space on your phone where applications, images, movies, and other things are kept. Having adequate storage guarantees your phone can install new applications, record memories, and perform properly.

Battery Life: The battery life dictates how long you can use your phone on a single charge. Battery capacity varies based on use habits and settings. Understanding how to manage battery life is vital for getting the most out of your iQOO Z9x.

Optimizing Performance for Everyday Tasks

Here are some ways to guarantee your iQOO Z9x runs best for daily tasks:

Managing Background programmes: Background programmes running undetected might drain resources and possibly slow down your phone. Close applications you're not actively using by swiping them up from the recent apps panel. Consider employing features like "App power management" or "Background app refresh control" (options could vary based on your phone's model) to reduce background activity for less commonly used applications.

Regular App Updates: App developers routinely issue updates that contain bug repairs, performance enhancements, and new features. Keeping your applications updated provides optimum performance and security for your phone. Update applications periodically via the Google Play Store.

Smart Storage Management: Your phone's storage capacity might fill up rapidly, thus harming performance. Regularly examine your storage use and consider eliminating superfluous files, images, or movies. You may also leverage utilities like "Storage Cleaner" (if available) to locate and clear temporary or garbage files that collect over time.

Disabling Unnecessary Animations: Subtle animations may give a touch of refinement to your phone's user interface. However, they may also consume resources. Explore your phone's settings to see whether options like "Reduce animations" or "Developer options" (may take extra steps to enable) allow you to eliminate or decrease animations for a possibly smoother user experience.

Extending Battery Life Using Power Saving Features

Modern cellphones provide different functions to optimise battery life. Let's investigate various strategies to prolong your iQOO Z9x's battery life:

Understanding Battery Usage: Navigate to your phone's battery settings to see which applications and functionalities drain the most juice. This information helps you to find areas for optimization. Look for choices like "Battery usage" or "Battery optimization."

Enabling power Saver Mode: Most phones provide a "Battery Saver Mode" that minimises background activity, restricts app refresh rates, and improves performance to preserve power. Activating Battery Saver Mode is an easy technique to prolong battery life when your phone is running low.

Adjusting Screen Brightness: The display is a huge power drain. Reducing screen brightness is a simple but efficient approach to preserve battery life. You may change screen brightness manually either the quick settings panel or inside the display settings menu. Some phones include capabilities like "Adaptive brightness" that automatically modify screen brightness depending on ambient light conditions.

Optimizing Location Services: Location services are vital for certain applications, but continually running them in the background might deplete your battery. Navigate to your location settings and modify permissions for applications to access location services. Only allow location access to applications that actually need it.

Bluetooth and Wi-Fi Management: When not in use, consider deactivating Bluetooth and Wi-Fi to preserve power. These capabilities continually look for connections, and deactivating them when not required will dramatically increase battery life. You can rapidly turn Bluetooth and Wi-Fi on/off using the fast settings panel.

Night Mode (if available): Some iQOO Z9x models could have a "Night Mode" that alters the screen color temperature to warmer tones at night. This can be easier on the eyes in low-light conditions and could also contribute marginally to increased battery life.

By understanding the elements that effect performance and adopting these optimization suggestions, you can guarantee your iQOO Z9x performs smoothly and efficiently for all your everyday chores. Remember, optimization is a constant effort. Experiment with various settings and features to find what works best for your specific use habits.

Beyond the Basics: Advanced Performance Optimization (Optional)

For consumers trying to wring every ounce of performance out of their iQOO Z9x, here are some advanced optimization techniques:

Developer Options (use with caution): Your phone can include hidden "Developer options" with sophisticated settings that might impair performance. Enable these options at your own risk, since certain settings could cause unexpected behavior if not utilised appropriately. Consult a trusted source or internet forums before altering developer settings.

Custom Kernel/ROMs (extreme users only): Advanced users may dig into altering the phone's core software (kernel) or installing custom ROMs (alternative operating systems). This is a complicated procedure with significant hazards, so only undertake it if you possess the technical skills and understand the potential implications.

It's vital to realise that these complex approaches are not suggested for casual users. The advantages could be minor for regular work, and there's a danger of adding instability or security flaws.

CHAPTER 9

Security and Privacy - Protecting Your Data and Maintaining Control

Your iQOO Z9x contains a plethora of personal information, from contacts and messages to images and financial statistics. This chapter offers you with the skills to encrypt your smartphone, manage app permissions, and surf the web securely, safeguarding your privacy and preserving your precious data.

Setting Up Screen Lock and Other Security Measures

The first line of protection for your iQOO Z9x is a powerful screen lock. This prevents illegal access to your device and preserves your information.

Enabling Screen Lock: Navigate to your phone's security settings. Look for settings like "Screen lock," "Lock screen," or "Device security." You'll be offered with multiple screen lock techniques, each giving a different degree of security:

Swipe: Easy to use but gives limited security.

Pin : A numerical code needs remembering a series of numbers.

Pattern: Draw a particular pattern on the screen for unlocking.

Password: Offers greater intricacy than a PIN utilising a mix of characters, numbers, and symbols.

Fingerprint (if available): Uses your fingerprint for safe and easy unlocking.

Face Unlock (if available): Uses facial recognition technology for unlocking with your face (be advised that this technique could be less secure than fingerprint or password).

Choosing the Right Lock mechanism: Consider the balance between security and convenience when picking a screen lock mechanism. A strong PIN, password, or fingerprint gives the greatest security for your data. Fingerprint and Face Unlock are handy but can be less secure than complicated passwords.

Additional Security Measures:

Beyond screen lock, examine additional security measures your phone can offer:

Find My Device: Enables remote location monitoring and data cleaning in case your phone is misplaced or stolen. (Requires a Google account established).

Secure Startup (if available): Requires inputting your PIN, password, or fingerprint even after restarting your phone, adding an extra degree of protection.

App encryption: Encrypts app data for greater security (availability can vary on your unique model).

Managing App Permissions and Data Privacy

Modern applications routinely seek access to numerous functionalities and data on your phone. Here's how to control app permissions and safeguard your privacy:

Understanding App Permissions: When you install an app, it could seek permission to use features like your location, camera, microphone, contacts, storage, etc. Granting permission enables the programme to perform as intended. However, it's vital to be aware of what permissions you provide.

Reviewing App Permissions

Navigate to your phone's app settings. Look for choices like "App permissions" or "Permissions manager." This area enables you to check and adjust permissions given to particular applications.

Granting Permissions Wisely

Only provide permissions that are needed for the app's operation. For example, a flashlight app doesn't require access to your location. Deny permissions that appear unneeded or unrelated to the app's purpose.

Privacy Settings: Your phone's settings likely have a distinct "Privacy" area. Explore these options to customise things including location services, app activity monitoring, and targeted advertising. You may alter these options to restrict how much data applications can gather and how it's utilised.

Using Secure Browsing Practices

The internet provides a plethora of information and tools, but it also contains significant security dangers. Here are some suggestions for safe surfing on your iQOO Z9x:

Using a trustworthy Browser: Download and use a trustworthy web browser from the Google Play Store. Popular alternatives include Google Chrome, Mozilla Firefox, and Samsung Internet (depending on your model). These browsers stress security and include features like phishing prevention and virus blocking.

Beware of Phishing Links: Phishing scams seek to fool you into exposing personal information or clicking on dangerous links. Be careful of emails, text messages, or websites that look strange. Never submit personal information on websites you don't know.

Keeping Your Browser Updated: Browser upgrades typically contain security patches and bug fixes. Regularly upgrade your browser via the Google Play Store to guarantee you have the latest security protection.

Downloading from trustworthy Sources: Only download applications and files from trustworthy sources like the Google Play Store. Downloading from unknown websites might expose your phone to malware or viruses.

Public Wi-Fi Security: Public Wi-Fi networks are handy, but they might be less safe than private networks. Avoid accessing personal information or bank accounts when connecting to public Wi-Fi. Consider utilising a VPN (Virtual Private Network) for an additional layer of protection on public Wi-Fi networks (see to Chapter 5 for a short description of VPNs).

Strong Passwords and Authentication: Use strong and unique passwords for all your online accounts. A password manager can help you generate and maintain complicated passwords securely. Avoid using the same password for numerous accounts. Be aware of websites or applications demanding unnecessary personal information during registration. Enable two-factor authentication (2FA) wherever feasible for an extra layer of protection for your online accounts. 2FA normally includes entering a code texted to your phone in addition to your password when signing in.

By applying these security steps, maintaining app permissions, and following safe surfing habits, you may greatly lower the chance of data breaches, malware infections, and other security concerns on your iQOO Z9x. Remember, attentiveness is crucial. keep updated on the newest security threats and regularly upgrade your knowledge and security procedures to keep ahead of any issues.

Conclusion

Security and privacy are crucial in today's digital environment. By following the directions in this chapter, you've provided yourself with the skills to safeguard your iQOO Z9x, control app permissions, and surf the web securely. With a mix of knowledge and proactive actions, you can guarantee your phone stays a safe and secure refuge for your personal information and online activities. Now that you've examined several features of your iQOO Z9x, you're well on your way to mastering your gadget and unlocking its full potential. Enjoy exploring the fascinating world of mobile technology with confidence and peace of mind

CHAPTER 10

Going Beyond the Basics - Tips and Tricks for Power Users

You've grasped the foundations of your iQOO Z9x, but there's always more to explore. This chapter looks into advanced features, customization choices, and hidden gems to boost your user experience and unleash the full potential of your phone.

Utilizing Google Assistant for Everyday Tasks

Google Assistant, your built-in virtual assistant, is a great tool for simplifying everyday activities and improving productivity. Here's how to exploit its capabilities:

Voice Commands: Activate Google Assistant with a simple voice command like "Hey Google" or "Ok Google" (customization options could be available). Once engaged, use your voice to manage your phone, ask inquiries, or give instructions.

Hands-Free Convenience: Google Assistant provides hands-free interaction with your phone. Make calls, send messages, play music, set alarms, or navigate with voice commands. This is especially beneficial when driving, cooking, or doing other duties that occupy your hands.

Information Retrieval: Need rapid answers? Google Assistant may be your own search engine. Ask inquiries about anything, receive weather updates, check sports scores, or translate languages, all with voice commands.

Smart Home Integration (if applicable): If your iQOO Z9x supports smart home integration, you can operate compatible smart devices like lights, thermostats, or appliances with voice commands via Google Assistant.

Reminders and Notes: Set reminders for future events, make shopping lists, or dictate notes using Google Assistant. This guarantees you remain organized and never miss critical duties.

By exploring these functions, you'll find Google Assistant as a helpful tool for optimising your daily routine and enhancing your productivity on your iQOO Z9x.

Split-Screen Functionality and Multitasking

Modern cellphones are multitasking powerhouses. Your iQOO Z9x provides split-screen capabilities, letting you operate with two programmes concurrently.

Activating Split-Screen: The procedure for activating split-screen could vary somewhat based on your phone type. Here's a general approach:

- Open the first app you wish to use in split-screen mode.
- Navigate to the recent applications screen (usually by sliding up from the bottom of the screen and holding).
- Look for a split-screen icon (typically represented by two rectangles) adjacent to the app preview you wish to utilise in the first half of the screen.
- Tap the split-screen icon and pick the second app you wish to utilise in the bottom half of the screen.

Resizing Split-Screen Windows: You may alter the size of each app window in split-screen mode by dragging the dividing line between them.

App Compatibility: Not all applications are suited for split-screen capability. You could face restrictions with some applications.

Split-screen multitasking lets you surf the web while taking notes, check social media while replying to emails, or execute various combinations of work concurrently, boosting your productivity on the iQOO Z9x.

Hidden Features and Customization Options

Your iQOO Z9x can hide secret functions and customization possibilities waiting to be uncovered. Let's investigate some possible gems:

Developer Options (use with caution):
As discussed in Chapter 8, your phone can include hidden "Developer options" including advanced settings. Enable these options at your own risk, since certain settings may impair functionality or stability if not used appropriately. Consult a trusted source or internet forums before altering developer settings. These settings could include functionality like enabling USB debugging or altering display animation rates.

Navigation Gestures: Standard navigation keys (back, home, recent applications) are recognisable, but your phone could feature other navigation gestures for a more simplified experience. Explore your settings to discover whether features like swiping motions for navigation are available.

One-Handed Mode: Using your phone with one hand might be tough. Some iQOO Z9x versions could have a "One-handed mode" that reduces the screen display to a more manageable size for single-handed operation. Explore your settings to check whether this option is accessible.

Customizing the Lock Screen and Wallpaper: Personalize your phone's look by setting a custom wallpaper or lock screen picture. You may select from pre-loaded alternatives or use your own photographs. Explore your display settings to obtain these possibilities.

Notification Customization: Fine-tune how your phone tells you about texts, calls, and app changes. Set notification sounds, modify notification priority, or mute alerts from particular applications .

Taking Screenshots and Screen Recording: Capture screenshots or record your phone's screen for numerous uses. Typically, holding the power button and volume down button simultaneously snaps a screenshot. Your phone could also provide unique options for screen recording under the quick settings panel or using specific gestures.

Digital Wellbeing tools: Modern smartphones include tools that help you regulate your phone use habits. Explore "Digital Wellbeing" options (name could change) to monitor app consumption, set time restrictions for certain applications, or plan downtime to disengage from your phone.

Accessibility Features: Your phone likely has several accessibility features to boost usability for individuals with impairments. Explore the accessibility options to find capabilities like text-to-speech, magnification gestures, or high contrast themes.

Customizing Sounds and Vibrations: Personalize your phone's sound experience by creating custom ringtones, notification sounds, and altering vibration patterns. This lets you adapt your phone's audio to your liking.

Dark Mode (if available): Some iQOO Z9x models could have a "Dark Mode" that transforms the entire colour scheme to darker tones. This may be easier on the eyes in low-light conditions and could also contribute marginally to enhanced battery life (as described in Chapter 8).

By digging into these secret features and customization choices, you can customise your iQOO Z9x and fit it to your individual tastes and use patterns. Remember, examining your phone's settings and playing with various options is crucial to unlocking its full potential and creating a user experience that precisely meets your requirements.

CHAPTER 11

Troubleshooting Common Issues

Even the most powerful systems may face occasional glitches. This chapter supplies you with answers for typical difficulties you can experience with your iQOO Z9x, helping you troubleshoot connection problems, resolve app crashes, and resuscitate an unresponsive phone.

Addressing Connectivity Problems

Unable to Connect: Ensure Wi-Fi is enabled on your phone.

Verify you're typing the right Wi-Fi password.
Restart your phone and router/modem.
Forget the Wi-Fi network on your phone and rejoin.
Check for router/modem firmware upgrades (see your router/modem handbook for details).

Slow Wi-Fi: Move closer to the Wi-Fi router to enhance signal strength.
Consider interference from other wireless devices. Disable unneeded background programmes that could drain bandwidth.
 Contact your internet service provider (ISP) if the situation continues.

Mobile Data Issues:

 Unable to Connect: Ensure mobile data is enabled in your settings.
 Check your mobile data plan with your provider and ensure you have adequate data.

Check for network coverage difficulties in your region (call your carrier).

Slow Mobile Data: Move to a location with greater signal strength. Disable unneeded background programmes that could drain data.

Contact your carrier to determine if there are any network difficulties or limits on your plan.

Bluetooth Issues:

Pairing Problems: Ensure Bluetooth is enabled on both devices.

Make sure the device you wish to link with is discoverable.

Forget previously linked Bluetooth devices on your phone and attempt pairing again. Restart your phone and the Bluetooth device.

Connection Drops: Move closer to the Bluetooth device for a better connection.

Ensure there's no interference from other wireless devices.

Restart your phone and the Bluetooth device.

Update the Bluetooth software on your phone (if available).

By following these instructions, you can efficiently resolve common connection difficulties and guarantee your iQOO Z9x remains connected flawlessly.

Fixing App Crashes and Performance Issues

Force Close the App: Navigate to your phone's app settings and identify the troublesome app.

Look for the "Force Stop" option and touch on it to forcibly shut the app.

This may occasionally fix temporary difficulties.

Restart Your Phone: A simple restart will typically alleviate temporary memory difficulties and cure app crashes.

Update the App: Outdated applications could face compatibility difficulties. Open the Google Play Store and check for updates for the malfunctioning app.

Clear App Cache: The app cache contains temporary data that might collect over time and possibly lead to troubles. Navigate to your app settings, pick the affected programme, and seek for an option to "Clear Cache." Be warned that deleting the cache could need you to log in again to certain applications.

Reinstall the App: If the problem continues, try uninstalling and reinstalling the app. This removes all app data and settings, so ensure you back up any vital information inside the app before removing.

Performance Issues:

Close Unnecessary Background applications: Background applications may drain resources and slow down your phone. Close any applications you're not actively using by swiping them up from the recent apps panel.

Disable Unnecessary Animations: Subtle animations might give a bit of elegance, but they can also drain resources. Explore your phone's settings to see whether options like "Reduce animations" or "Developer options" (may take extra steps to enable) allow you to eliminate or decrease animations for a possibly smoother user experience.

Free Up Storage Space: Insufficient storage space might hinder performance. Review your storage utilisation and consider eliminating superfluous files, images, or movies. You may also leverage utilities like

"Storage Cleaner" (if available) to locate and clear temporary or garbage files.

Update Your Phone's Software: Software updates frequently bring bug fixes and performance enhancements. Check for and install any available software updates for your iQOO Z9x from the settings menu.

By following these methods, you may fix frequent app crashes and performance concerns, ensuring your iQOO Z9x operates smoothly and effectively.

What to Do If Your Phone Doesn't Respond

If your iQOO Z9x becomes entirely unresponsive and won't switch off or react to touch, a hard restart is recommended. The technique for forcing a restart could vary somewhat based on your individual phone model, but here's a basic approach:

Locate the Power Button and Volume Buttons:

Identify the physical buttons on your phone: the power button and the volume buttons (up and down).

Press and Hold the Buttons: Simultaneously press and hold the power button and a volume button (usually the volume down button) for at least 10-15 seconds. Ignore any prompts that may display on the screen throughout this procedure.

Wait for the Restart: Your phone should vibrate and then show the iQOO logo, signifying a successful restart.

Release the Buttons: Once the iQOO logo displays, you may securely release the buttons. Your phone will start up properly.

If the Forced Restart Doesn't Work:

In rare circumstances, a forced restart may not address the problem. Here are some extra actions to consider:

Connect to Charger: If your phone's battery is fully exhausted, it could not reply. Connect your phone to a charger and wait for it to charge for at least 30 minutes before trying another forced restart.

Contact Customer service: If none of the troubleshooting procedures work, it's suggested to contact iQOO customer service for more help. They may be able to identify the issue and give a remedy, or recommend bringing your phone in for repair.

Important Note:

Before doing a hard restart, check you haven't unintentionally hit and held the power button, which can activate the Google

Assistant. Briefly pushing the power button should wake the screen and enable you to unlock your phone normally. A forced restart is only required when your phone is entirely unusable.

By following these instructions, you can successfully resolve common difficulties with your iQOO Z9x and guarantee it continues to perform properly. Remember, if you face difficulties beyond your abilities to fix, don't hesitate to reach out to iQOO customer service for professional help.

This chapter has provided you with the knowledge to solve typical difficulties you can experience with your iQOO Z9x. From managing connection difficulties and correcting app crashes to recovering an unresponsive phone, you've acquired vital skills to maintain maximum performance and a flawless user experience. With this thorough guide at your disposal, you can confidently handle any issues that occur and maintain your iQOO Z9x working at its best. Now that you've investigated many areas of your phone and possess the expertise to solve typical difficulties, you're well-equipped to tackle the fascinating world of mobile technology with your iQOO Z9x.

CHAPTER 12

Taking Care of Your iQOO Z9x

Your iQOO Z9x is a wonderful investment. By adopting correct maintenance methods, you may prolong its longevity, maintain optimal performance, and assure a great user experience for years to come. This chapter includes critical guidelines for charging your phone properly, safeguarding it from physical harm, and keeping it clean and functioning.

Proper Charging Practices and Battery Maintenance

Your iQOO Z9x likely employs a Lithium-ion (Li-ion) battery. Here are some basic strategies to enhance battery life and health:

Use the Included Charger and Cable: Whenever feasible, use the charging adaptor and cable that comes with your phone. These are intended to function best with your iQOO Z9x, providing safe and efficient charging.

Avoid Extreme Temperatures: Extreme heat or cold might harm your battery. Avoid keeping your phone in direct sunlight for lengthy periods or exposing it to frigid temperatures.

Don't Let the Battery entirely Drain: It's advisable to recharge your phone before the battery entirely depletes.

Avoid Overnight Charging: While occasional overnight charging won't degrade your battery considerably, it's typically advisable to disconnect your phone once it hits 100%. Modern phones frequently have built-in mechanisms to optimize charging and avoid overcharging.

Charging Habits and App Usage: Certain programmes and background operations might drain more battery power. Monitor your battery consumption in your phone's settings and detect applications that drain the power unnecessarily. Consider closing such applications while not in use or modifying their settings to minimise battery usage.

Software upgrades: Software upgrades typically feature enhancements for battery performance. Keeping your phone's software up-to-date may contribute to enhanced battery life.

By following these methods, you may prolong your iQOO Z9x's battery life and guarantee it continues to work ideally over time. Remember, batteries are consumable components, and their capacity will gradually diminish with continuous usage. If you detect a substantial loss in battery life even after following these instructions, consider changing the battery (if user-replaceable) or contacting iQOO customer care for servicing alternatives.

Protecting Your Phone with a Case and Screen Protector

Your iQOO Z9x is a stylish gadget, yet accidents happen. A case and screen protector give important protection against scratches, bumps, and drops.

Choosing the Right Case: There are several case designs and materials available, each giving varying degrees of protection and beauty. Consider aspects including your lifestyle, required amount of protection, and personal tastes when purchasing a case.

Durable Materials: Cases built from TPU (thermoplastic polyurethane), silicone, or robust materials like polycarbonate give excellent impact protection.

Slim vs. Rugged Protection: Slim cases provide a mix between protection and preserving a small profile for comfortable daily usage. Rugged cases give more comprehensive protection but might be heavier.

Screen Protectors: Applying a tempered glass screen protector preserves your iQOO Z9x's display from scratches, fingerprints.

Case and Screen Protector Compatibility: Ensure your selected case and screen protector are compatible with your exact iQOO Z9x model to ensure a flawless fit and best protection.

Investing in a premium case and screen protector is a sensible move to keep your iQOO Z9x from regular wear and tear, maintaining its perfect state and functioning.

Cleaning and Maintaining Your Device

Keeping your iQOO Z9x clean not only improves its look but may help avoid future issues:

Cleaning the Screen: Use a soft, microfiber towel to wipe off the screen. Avoid using abrasive materials or strong chemicals that might harm the display coating. Slightly dampen the cloth with water for persistent smudges, but avoid excessive dampness.

Ports and Buttons: Dust or debris may build in ports and buttons, affecting functioning. Use a soft brush or compressed air to carefully clean these spots. Never introduce sharp items into any ports.

Device Body: The phone's back and sides may be wiped with a gentle, microfiber cloth. If you use a case, remove it frequently for thorough cleaning of both the cover and the phone itself. Avoid using any cleaning solutions directly on the phone's body.

Avoid Moisture Exposure: Your iQOO Z9x could have some water resistance (see to your user manual for precise specifics). However, it's normally preferable to avoid exposing it to excessive dampness, dust, or sand.

Software Maintenance: Regularly upgrading your phone's software is critical for ensuring maximum performance and security. Software updates sometimes contain bug fixes, performance enhancements, and security patches. Enable automatic software updates whenever feasible, or check for updates manually in your phone's settings.

App Management: Uninstalling unneeded programmes may free up storage space and perhaps enhance speed. Additionally, examine app permissions and deactivate unneeded access for applications to defend your privacy and battery life.

Declutter Your Home Screen: Excessive widgets and app icons on your home screen may clutter your interface and slow down performance. Organize your home screen by establishing folders for relevant applications and deleting unneeded widgets.

Data Backups: Regularly back up your vital data like images, contacts, and messages to a cloud storage service or external storage device. This assures you don't lose vital information in case of unforeseen situations.

By following these cleaning and maintenance procedures, you can keep your iQOO Z9x working smoothly and looking its best for a long time. Remember, a little care goes a long way in protecting the life and functionality of your important gadget.

Conclusion

This chapter has armed you with the information to properly care for your iQOO Z9x. From applying correct charging methods and battery care to securing your phone with a case and screen protector, and maintaining cleanliness and software health, you now know the skills to guarantee your iQOO Z9x stays a dependable and fun companion for years to come. With a mix of knowledge and proactive maintenance, you can optimise the lifetime and performance of your iQOO Z9x, letting you to fully embrace the possibilities of your mobile technology. Congratulations! You've successfully navigated our thorough guide to mastering your iQOO Z9x. Now go on your mobile adventure with confidence, armed with the knowledge and abilities to unleash the full potential of your smartphone.

CONCLUSION

Summary and Looking Forward

Congratulations! You've reached the finish of our detailed guide on mastering your iQOO Z9x. Throughout your trip, you've dug into numerous parts of your phone, from the foundations of setup and navigation to exploring advanced capabilities and fixing frequent faults. This last chapter serves as a recap of the important lessons and gives a look into the amazing possibilities that lie ahead with your iQOO Z9x.

A Recap of Your Learning Journey

Getting Started (Chapter 1 & 2): You started by setting up your iQOO Z9x, familiarizing yourself with the hardware, navigating the user interface, and making important changes. You examined key capabilities including making calls, sending messages, accessing the web, and managing applications.

Unveiling the Power Within (Chapter 3 & 4): You delved deeper into the world of multimedia, discovering how to capture stunning photos and videos using the camera app, exploring creative editing options, and enjoying immersive entertainment experiences through multimedia playback and gaming features. You also learnt about connecting to Wi-Fi networks, managing Bluetooth connections, and transferring data using different techniques.

customising and Efficiency (Chapter 5 & 6): You investigated customising options to suit your iQOO Z9x experience to your tastes. This includes personalising the home screen, alerts, and audio. You also found productivity advantages like split-screen multitasking, controlling alerts, and employing Google Assistant for hands-free support. These technologies help you optimise your process and enhance productivity.

Staying Secure and Connected (Chapter 7, 8 & 9): You learnt the significance of cybersecurity and data privacy. You discussed strategies for setting up powerful screen locks and regulating app permissions to secure your information. Understanding safe surfing behaviours and keeping your software updated were also addressed. Additionally, you got insights on improving battery life for extended use.

Unlocking secret Gems (Chapter 10): You explored beyond the fundamentals, uncovering secret features and customization choices that customise your iQOO Z9x experience. Utilizing Google Assistant for different tasks, mastering split-screen multitasking, and exploring one-handed mode were just some of the key abilities you gained.

Troubleshooting Like a Pro (Chapter 11): You got the ability to troubleshoot typical difficulties you could experience with your iQOO Z9x. This includes correcting connection difficulties, repairing app crashes, and resurrecting an unresponsive phone. By following these procedures, you can maintain maximum performance and guarantee a pleasant user experience.

Taking Care of Your Investment (Chapter 12): You studied optimal charging procedures to enhance battery life. Understanding the need of utilising a case and screen protector to prevent your phone from physical harm was also addressed. Regular cleaning and software maintenance were emphasised as key measures for guaranteeing long-lasting performance and a flawless look for your iQOO Z9x.

Looking Forward: A World of Possibilities

Now that you've mastered the foundations and unlocked advanced features, a world of possibilities awaits with your iQOO Z9x. Here are a few fascinating avenues to explore:

Mobile Photography and Videography: Your iQOO Z9x's camera capabilities can be further enhanced by exploring professional shooting modes, learning creative editing techniques, and utilizing various camera apps to capture unique perspectives and stunning visuals.

Exploring the App Universe: The Google Play Store offers a vast library of apps catering to diverse interests. From productivity tools and social media platforms to educational apps and mobile games, there's an app for practically anything. Explore different categories, discover hidden gems, and personalize your app collection to enhance your mobile experience.

Staying Connected and Informed: Your iQOO Z9x keeps you connected with loved ones through messaging apps and social media, but it also serves as a window to the world. Stay informed with news apps, explore educational resources online, or delve into the world of podcasts and audiobooks. The possibilities for staying connected and learning are endless.

Embracing the Mobile Lifestyle: Utilize location-based services for navigation and exploration. Mobile banking apps offer convenient financial management options. Fitness apps can help you stay active and achieve your health goals. Your iQOO Z9x can seamlessly integrate into your daily life, making it easier, more efficient, and more enjoyable.

A Final Note: Continuous Learning

The world of technology is constantly evolving. New features, updates, and innovations emerge regularly. Don't hesitate to explore online resources, forums, and communities dedicated to your iQOO Z9x model. Stay updated with the latest software releases and keep learning to unlock the full potential of your device. Remember, the journey of mastering your iQOO Z9x is an ongoing process. Embrace the learning experience, explore new functionalities, and allow your creativity to flourish as you navigate the exciting world of mobile technology.

With this comprehensive guide as your companion, you're well-equipped to embark on your mobile adventure with confidence. May your iQOO Z9x become a valuable tool for communication, creativity, productivity, and exploration. We hope you've enjoyed this journey of learning and discovery!

APPENDIX

This appendix serves as a helpful resource for additional investigation and clarification of ideas linked to your iQOO Z9x. It gives a selected selection of extra resources and a complete vocabulary to expand your comprehension and equip you to navigate the world of mobile technology with confidence.

Additional Resources

Official iQOO Website: The official iQOO website is a fantastic resource for acquiring the latest information on your phone. You may discover user manuals, software update information, troubleshooting instructions, and customer help choices. Look for the particular webpage matching to your location for localized material.

iQOO User Forums: Online user forums devoted to iQOO devices may be a treasure source of knowledge and assistance. These forums enable you to interact with other iQOO Z9x users, exchange experiences, ask questions, and seek solutions to common difficulties. Search online for relevant iQOO user forums for your location.

Android Central: Android Central is a renowned website giving extensive information for Android devices, including the iQOO Z9x. You may discover news articles, tutorials, reviews, and troubleshooting instructions to expand your knowledge of the Android operating system and its features.

YouTube Tutorials: Many useful video tutorials may be available on YouTube that illustrate certain features of the iQOO Z9x.

Search for tutorials pertaining to your phone model and desired tasks to obtain visual help.

Online Tech journals: Several online tech journals provide in-depth reviews, comparisons, and news items regarding mobile phones. Reading such publications may give vital insights on the capabilities of your iQOO Z9x and its place within the greater smartphone ecosystem.

By accessing these resources, you may remain current on the newest advancements relating to your iQOO Z9x, find new tips and tricks, and interact with a community of other users.

Glossary

Android: The operating system powering your iQOO Z9x. It's a mobile operating system created by Google and utilised on a broad variety of smartphones and tablets.

App (Application): A self-contained software application meant to do certain functions on your phone, such as games, social networking platforms, or productivity tools.

Battery Life: The length of time your phone can work on a single charge.

Bluetooth: A wireless technology that enables your phone to connect to external devices like headsets, speakers, or other smartphones for data transmission or music streaming.

CPU (Central Processing Unit): The brain of your phone, responsible for processing data and commands.

Data: The information exchanged or saved on your phone, such as images, videos, messages, and app data.

GB (Gigabyte): A unit of storage capacity on your phone.

GPS (Global Positioning technology): A satellite-based navigation technology that enables your phone to identify its position.

Home Screen: The main screen of your phone where you find app icons, widgets, and shortcuts for easy access to commonly used features.

Hotspot: A function that converts your phone into a portable Wi-Fi router, enabling other devices to access the internet over your phone's data connection.

Launcher: The software programme responsible for maintaining your home screen layout and launching applications.

RAM (Random Access Memory): Temporary memory utilised by your phone to store previously accessed data and apps for quicker performance.

ROM (Read-Only Memory): The permanent storage on your phone that stores the operating system, applications, and your personal data.

Software: The collection of instructions that teaches your phone's hardware how to work.

Storage: The capacity available on your phone to hold applications, images, movies, and other data.

USB (Universal Serial Bus): A port used for charging your phone and exchanging data between your phone and a computer or other devices.

User Interface (UI): The visual components and layout that you interact with on your phone's screen.

VPN (Virtual Private Network): A technology that provides a secure encrypted tunnel between your phone and the internet, safeguarding your online privacy and perhaps providing access to geo-restricted material.

Wi-Fi: A wireless networking technology that enables your phone to connect to the internet via a router or hotspot.

This glossary includes meanings for common phrases you could meet when using your iQOO Z9x and exploring the world of mobile technology. By learning these terminologies, you may explore your phone's capabilities with more comfort and confidence.

Additional Notes

This lexicon is not comprehensive, and new terminology may develop as technology progresses. Don't hesitate to use internet resources or search engines for definitions of strange terminology you discover.

Software upgrades could offer new features or change current functions. Refer to the official iQOO website or user manuals for the latest information regarding your individual iQOO Z9x model.

The mobile technology environment is continually evolving. New features, applications, and innovations are added periodically. Embrace the spirit of continuous learning to keep updated and experience the ever-expanding possibilities afforded by your iQOO Z9x.

We hope this appendix has acted as a beneficial resource for your mobile journey. With the information obtained from this tutorial and the supplementary resources offered, you are well-equipped to tackle the fascinating world of mobile technology and unleash the full potential of your iQOO Z9x.